C000193846

Weekend Walks West of Reading

Short Scenic Strolls For All Ages
in West Berks and South Oxon

John Prior

Nine Peas Publishing

Published by Nine Peas Publishing

First published 2014
Updated and reprinted 2017

© John Prior 2017

All rights reserved. No part of this book may be reproduced
in any form or by any means without the permission
of the owner of the copyright.

Steam train photograph on page 19 © Matthew Ring
Bird photographs on page 35 © PhotoSpin.com
All other photographs © John Prior or Chris Preston

ISBN 978-0-9929688-1-6

Designed by Chris Preston

Typeset by Chris Preston

Printed by Press to Print Reading Ltd

Weekend Walks
West of Reading

Short Scenic Strolls For All Ages in West Berks and South Oxon

PUBLISHER'S NOTE
Whilst great care has been taken to provide information about
the route, facilities and public transport for each walk that is accurate at
the time of publication, the publisher cannot be held responsible for
any inaccuracies or changes. However, feedback and updated
information from readers is welcomed, for any future editions
(email:ninepeaspublishing@btinternet.com). The sketch maps that
accompany the walks show only the main paths, roads and buildings
referred to in the route notes; Ordnance Survey maps provide
fuller information. All distances are approximate.

The cover photographs, clockwise from top left, are :
Whitchurch Mill pond and St Mary's Church (walk 8)
West Ilsley pond (walk 12)
Goring Lock (walk 6)
Cob walls at Blewbury (walk 3)
Approaching Mapledurham Lock (walk 9)
Near Bower Farm, Aldworth (walk 2)

Symbols used on maps

Walk Start	⬤
Toilets	🚹🚺
Café/Pub	☕
Playground	🎠
Viewpoint	☀
Railway Station	⇌

Contents

DEDICATION
To my wife Anne, daughters Jo, Cathy and Sarah
and grandchildren Ben, Josh, Hannah and Ethan.

ACKNOWLEDGEMENT and THANKS
To Chris for his patience and professionalism in
turning my typescript into this book.

Introduction

A few miles to the west of Reading lies a varied landscape of river valleys, villages, woods and gently rolling hills – almost all of it designated as an 'area of outstanding natural beauty'. It is easily accessible for walkers, being criss-crossed by miles of footpaths and bridleways. These 12 circular walks have been chosen for anyone who wants to get out into the fresh air for a short, interesting stroll in this great countryside.

Each route is no more than 2 miles long, mainly level, and incorporates places of interest, stops for refreshments or a picnic and a children's playground. The starting points have been chosen for easy car parking and/or access by public transport. Numbers within the route descriptions link to facts and figures about places passed.

The walks will suit families with children and anyone who wants some exercise for an hour or so in interesting surroundings. So pick a route and head off to enjoy the 'outstanding natural beauty' of this area. Despite the title, it doesn't *have* to be at a weekend!

The author

For almost 40 years I've lived in Pangbourne, where my wife Anne and I brought up our three daughters. It was they who originally inspired this book. At weekends we were keen to explore the local countryside but any walk also had to be child-friendly - not too long and, if possible, including a playground and an ice cream! So we collected such routes. Time has moved on and now we have four grandchildren. Therefore the walks in this book were chosen with both the young and the not-so-young in mind!

Walk Locations

DIDCOT

• *Blewbury*

B4016

A417

• *West Ilsley*

Aldworth •

A34

• *Hampstead Norreys*

B4009

M4

J13

River Pang

Bucklebury •

A339

NEWBURY

• *Thatcham Lake*

A4

River Kennet

Miles

0 1 2 3 4 5

Cholsey

B4009

• *Goring-on-Thames*

B4526

B471

A4074

A329

River Thames

• *Pangbourne & Whitchurch*
• *Purley-on-Thames*

A340

A329

READING

J12

A4

Theale •

M4

• *Aldermaston Wharf*

3

1 WALK ONE : ALDERMASTON WHARF

A stroll along a busy stretch of the Kennet and Avon canal, with two locks, and an optional visit to the tranquil River Kennet.

START/PARKING: Car park (pay and display) at the Kennet and Avon Canal Visitor Centre, Wharfside off the A340 just north of the lifting bridge (Nat Grid Ref 41/603672, Postcode RG7 4JS). Alternative parking in nearby Station Road (roadside) and at Aldermaston station (pay & display)
PUBLIC TRANSPORT: Aldermaston rail station; Reading to Newbury buses along the A4
DISTANCE: 1 mile (1½ km) or 2 miles (3¼ km)
REFRESHMENTS: Tea Room at the Kennet and Avon Canal Visitor Centre (open Weds - Sun from 11am); Aldermaston Wharf Marina shop (open 8.30am to 5pm daily); The Butt Inn (www.thebuttinn.biz)
PUBLIC TOILETS: On north bank of the canal, about 50 metres upstream of the lifting bridge. Toilets also at the Visitor Centre Tea Room and the Butt Inn for customers
PATHS: Footpaths and roads; level and suitable for pushchairs on the shorter walk. The paths on the longer (River Kennet) walk are unsuitable for pushchairs and liable to be muddy after wet weather

THE ROUTES: The Canal Visitor Centre has a tea room and garden, and by the gate is an information board about the history of the canal ❶. From the Centre, turn right along the canal towpath to the lifting bridge and walk across the bridge. Then carefully cross the main road (A340) and take the towpath opposite to nearby Aldermaston Lock ❷, usually busy with boats in spring and summer. After watching any lock activity, re-trace your steps to the road and carefully cross it to Mill Lane. On the right, near the road sign, a path leads to a park with a playground for primary and pre-school children, an 'outdoor gym' for adults, seats and plenty of space for a picnic. The Butt Inn is nearby, on the other side of the A340.

For the shorter walk, re-trace your steps to cross the lifting bridge and turn right on to the canal towpath. After the Visitor Centre, pass the boats tied up at the wharf where on the left is a marina shop selling cold drinks and ice creams. The towpath leads to Padworth Lock ❸ with seats and further opportunities for watching folk 'messing about in boats'! Then re-trace your steps along the canal towpath to the start.

For the longer walk along the River Kennet, from the park return to Mill Lane and turn right into it. This stony, single track road leads past Alder Bridge school and cottages on your left. Continue through some trees to the end, ignoring a footpath to the right, to reach the timber-clad buildings of Padworth Mill. Here, take the footpath to the left to reach a tranquil stretch of the River Kennet. This path runs between the river on the right and a lake (former gravel pit) on the left. Shortly, there are glimpses of Padworth House, built in the late 1700s and now an independent secondary school, on the hillside to the right.

Cross the stile by Padworth Bridge and turn left on to the road (care is needed, as there is no footpath). Follow the road to cross another bridge, then turn left down to the canal towpath. This leads past Padworth Lock ❸ to Aldermaston Wharf (with a marina shop selling cold drinks and ice creams) and the start of the walk.

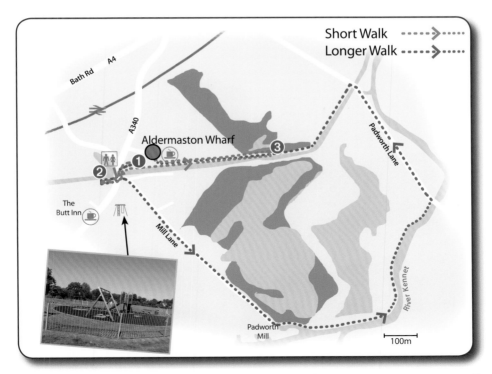

Facts and Figures

❶ The Kennet and Avon canal runs for 87 miles from Reading to Bristol. The River Kennet navigation from Reading to Newbury was opened in 1723 and the whole canal was completed in 1810. It was used for transporting goods to London and the Midlands including timber, malt, flour and cheese and the returning barges carried bulk goods such as coal and iron. The barges used were larger than standard canal narrow boats and a feature of the canal are the large locks. Competition from the Great Western Railway caused commercial traffic to decline and by the early 1950s much of the canal had fallen into disrepair. Following restoration, largely by volunteers, it re-opened fully in 1990.

❷ Aldermaston Lock was built between 1718 and 1723. One of 105 locks on the canal, it was originally turf-sided but was enlarged in the mid-18th century and given scalloped brick walls – a unique feature of this canal. These walls were raised in 1984 as part of lock restoration.

❸ Like the one at Aldermaston, Padworth Lock was turf-sided when first built in the early 18th century. During canal restoration in the 1980s, it was re-built as a brick lock and a commemorative plaque on the arm of one of the lock gates records donations that funded this.

Aldermaston basin & lifting bridge

Visitor Centre

Aldermaston Wharf

Explore this small village high in the Berkshire Downs, with an ancient church (the home of giants!) and great views.

START/PARKING: Roadside near the Village Hall in Bell Lane, off the B4009 Streatley to Newbury road (Nat Grid Ref 41/556796, Postcode RG8 9SE)
PUBLIC TRANSPORT: None available
DISTANCE: 1¼ miles (2 km) or 2 miles (3¼ km)
REFRESHMENTS: The Bell Inn, with a garden (closed Mondays, except BH)
PUBLIC TOILETS: None, but toilets at The Bell for customers
PATHS: Village roads and footpaths, liable to be muddy after wet weather; mainly level but with some gentle climbs. The paths are mostly unsuitable for pushchairs

THE ROUTES: The walk starts in Bell Lane, near the entrance to the Recreation Field which has benches, plenty of space for a picnic and, close to the Village Hall, a children's playground. Opened in summer 2013, this is suitable for younger primary and pre-school children.

Continue by taking the lane opposite the Bell Inn ❶, signed Compton and Hampstead Norreys. Keeping an eye open for any traffic, follow this gently downhill to reach the lychgate of St Mary's church ❷. Go through this into the churchyard, with its ancient yew. The church's main claim to fame are the 'Aldworth Giants' inside - children and adults alike will be fascinated by these nine sleeping figures from over 600 years ago.

After visiting the church, go past the yew to a gate in the corner and turn right into a by-way. This leads past Dumworth Farm on the left and then gently climbs into rolling farmland. These chalky downland fields are covered in flints and, as you climb, fine views open up to the right and back with Aldworth in the foreground and the hills of north Hampshire on the horizon. At the end of this track is a lane. For a shorter walk, turn right here to return to the village.

For a longer walk, turn left and follow the lane gently upwards as far as a by-way sign just after a farm entrance on the right. Turn right on to the by-way from which, at almost 600ft (185m) above sea level, there are far-reaching views. Follow this stony track down to a corner with a signpost for three by-ways. From here, part of the ancient Ridgeway ❸ can be seen in the middle distance, running uphill from right to left along a field boundary. Ahead and towards the right is the Thames valley, with the Chiltern Hills beyond.

Take the by-way that bears right at this corner, going through/over a gate towards Bower Farm. Fine views continue ahead and to the left. After about 100m, just beyond a gate, a footpath leads ahead into the farm. Ignore this path, taking the by-way to the left and follow the field edge towards another gate. Go through/over this gate and follow the track as it curves to the right, passing another by-way sign. There are more panoramic views towards Oxfordshire and the Chilterns to admire. Follow the track along a field edge for about 120m to a footpath sign on the right, where the boundary hedge changes direction. Then go through a gate on the right and take the footpath across the field towards a small wooded area. Pass through a gate into these woods and at the field edge beyond, turn right. Follow this path along the field edge for about 200m to where a path crosses it. Turn right here to cross a field and reach a path leading to the Recreation Field on the left and Bell Lane ahead.

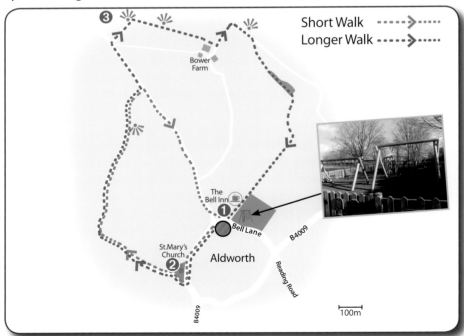

Facts and Figures

❶ The Bell Inn dates back to the 14th century and has been in the same family for over 250 years. It has a simple, unspoilt charm and has been voted CAMRA (real ale) 'pub of the year' on several occasions. Opposite is the old village well, 372ft (114m) deep and one of the deepest in England; piped water arrived in the village in 1914.

❷ The ancient St Mary's church is unique among English country churches because of its remarkable stone effigies – the 'Aldworth Giants'. These nine 'larger than life' figures represent five generations of the de la Beche family who were Lords of the Manor here until the mid-1300s. It is believed that their damaged condition results from a Cromwellian Act of Parliament in the mid-1600s that encouraged the destruction of such monuments. The church also contains the village's colourful Millennium tapestry. Outside is the Aldworth Yew, estimated to be at least 1000 years old. During a gale in January 1976, the trunk broke away but the root system survives.

❸ The Ridgeway is an ancient track, described as Britain's oldest road, running 43 miles from Overton Hill near Avebury, Wiltshire to the Thames at Streatley. It is now the western half of the Ridgeway National Trail, which continues to Ivinghoe Beacon in Buckinghamshire. For over 5000 years, this was part of a trading route stretching for about 250 miles from the Dorset coast to the Wash; the high, dry ground it followed made travel easy and provided a measure of protection by giving travellers a commanding view, warning against potential attacks.

St.Mary's Church

Sir Nicholas de la Beche

Two walks – one to discover this village of thatched cottages and clear streams, another going up into the Berkshire Downs to see panoramic views.

START/PARKING: Playground car park (free) in Bohams Road off the A417 on the western edge of Blewbury (Nat Grid Ref 41/ 525855, Postcode OX11 9HB)
PUBLIC TRANSPORT: Thames Travel buses from Didcot, Mon - Sat
DISTANCE: Village route 1½ miles (2½ km); Downs route 1¾ miles (3 km)
REFRESHMENTS: At Style Acre Tea Room, Savages Garden Centre (open to 4pm daily, see www.savagesblewbury.co.uk) and the Red Lion pub
PUBLIC TOILETS: None, but toilets at the Tea Room and the Red Lion for customers
PATHS: The Village route uses roads and footpaths, liable to be muddy after wet weather; mainly level and suitable for pushchairs. The Downs route involves a gentle climb and uneven paths that are muddy after wet weather and unsuitable for pushchairs

THE ROUTES: The walks start at the Blewbury Play Space, which has an interesting variety of wooden play equipment suitable for primary and secondary school children. The adjacent field has plenty of space for a picnic. Turn right down Bohams Road, to London Road where there is a garden centre and tea room opposite. Cross the road and turn right to pass Westbrook Street and reach Nottingham Fee where there are two walk options, the Village route and the Downs route.

VILLAGE ROUTE: To explore Blewbury - with its thatched cottages, streams, ancient church and cob walls - turn left into Nottingham Fee. Here there are thatched cottages and the 17th century Red Lion pub. Bear right just past the pub, to the end of Chapel Lane with the Methodist church on the right. The footpath ahead leads to a small lake called 'The Cleve' ❶ for which there is an information board on the left.

After viewing the lake, retrace your steps to Chapel Lane and take the path to the right, beside a cob wall topped with thatch ❷. The path leads to Church Road and ahead is St Michael's parish church ❸. Take the path to the right of the church, where there is an information board, and by the Rectory bear left into Church End. After crossing a clear stream (flowing from The Cleve) bear left to follow the road until it turns sharp left. A road at this corner leads to the Village Hall and Post Office, behind which there is a playground suitable for primary and pre-school children.

At the corner, turn left into Westbrook Street to pass a wooden barn then Boham's House on the left with its blue plaque recalling Kenneth Grahame ❹. Just beyond this, after a terrace of houses (part of Grahame Close), turn left down a gravel path bordered by a cob wall. This leads to Play Close village green, a shady area of grass with seats. Bear right across the grass to a path that crosses a stream. This path leads between cob walls to the Red Lion pub. Here, turn right into Nottingham Fee then almost immediately right again by thatched cottages. Follow this lane to where it becomes a footpath (Watery Lane), alongside and then crossing a clear, shallow stream. There are paddling opportunities here!

Turn left into Westbrook Street and then shortly right on to a footpath. Follow this towards open fields, until you come to a wooden gate in the hedge on the left. This leads into Savages Garden Centre, from where the start of the walk lies ahead along Bohams Road opposite. When Savages is closed, continue along the footpath to London Road and turn left to reach Bohams Road.

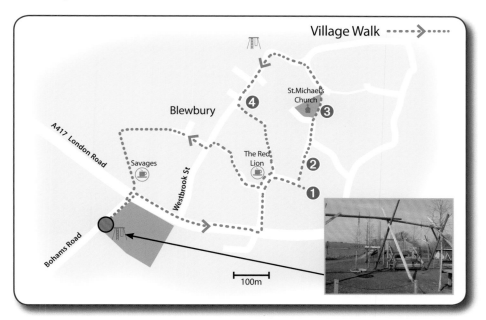

Village Walk ‑‑‑‑>‑‑‑‑

Blewbury

St.Michael's Church

Savages

The Red Lion

A417 London Road

Westbrook St

Bohams Road

100m

DOWNS ROUTE: For a walk up into the chalky Downs, turn right up the track opposite Nottingham Fee. Shortly, where this track bears right, continue ahead and up a short flight of steps on the left to follow the upper path. There is a gentle climb, soon passing the grassy mound of Blewbury Reservoir on the left. Where the upper and lower paths merge again, far-reaching views open up northwards over Blewbury towards Didcot and Wittenham Clumps. Continue ahead gently uphill to pass the gate to Lids Bottom, a wildlife site, on the left. About 200m beyond this, go through a gap in the hedge on the right to reach a farm track. Ahead is the summit of Churn Hill (160m high), with a reservoir shielded by trees.

Turn right on to the farm track (a permissive footpath) and follow this along the field edge. There are spectacular views over the Thames valley, with Wittenham Clumps in the middle distance and the Chilterns on the horizon to the right. The only sounds you may hear are skylarks and the wind! To the left, a mound topped by a metal post comes into view - this is Churn Knob ❺. By a gate at the field boundary, where the track runs downhill, turn right on to a bridleway. This also runs gently downhill, passing two seats that provide a convenient place to stop and admire the view. Continue downhill and the Play Space soon comes into view on the left. Go through a gap in the hedge on the left to cross the field and return to the car park.

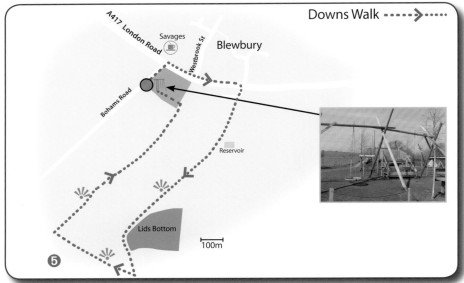

Facts and Figures

1 The Cleve is fed by 30 known springs, Blewbury lying on the 'spring line' at the foot of the chalky Berkshire Downs. This small lake is also known as the Watercress Beds, but the cultivation of watercress ceased in the late 1930s because of uncertain water flow and quality.

2 Cob walls are thought to have indicated ownership of land. They are made of clay, straw and mud, which is then whitewashed or painted, and thatched.

3 The parish church of St Michael and All Angels is Saxon in origin but was progressively enlarged, first by the Normans, up to the 15th century when the tower was added. Until the 1970s a curfew bell was rung each evening at 8pm, reputedly to guide travellers from the nearby Downs. In the churchyard, by the path leading to the south door, is a thought-provoking memorial to a George Napper who died in 1818.

4 From 1910 to 1920 Kenneth Grahame, the author of 'The Wind in the Willows', lived in Boham's House, Westbrook Street. He later moved to Church Cottage in Pangbourne where he lived until his death in 1932.

5 Churn Knob is the site of an ancient burial ground (barrow). In 634 AD, a Benedictine monk named Birinus was sent from Rome to convert the Midlands to Christianity. Cynegils, King of the West Saxons, invited Birinus to meet him at Churn Knob, a sacred place. He was successful in converting Cynegils and his people and was permitted to set up an abbey in Dorchester-on-Thames. In celebration, local churches organize a pilgrimage each mid-summer from Churn Knob to Dorchester (11 miles).

Nottingham Fee

Kenneth Grahame plaque

13

Visit this small village (now with Royal connections!) and the animals in a farm park, in the beautiful Pang valley.

START/PARKING: Car park at Bucklebury Recreation Ground, on an unclassified road about 3 miles north-east of Thatcham (Nat Grid Ref 41/552708, postcode RG7 6PR)
PUBLIC TRANSPORT: None available
DISTANCE: 1¼ miles (2 km)
REFRESHMENTS: Woody's Café and Tea Room, open 8.30am to 5pm daily, except 25 and 26 Dec – see www.buckleburyfarmpark.co.uk
PUBLIC TOILETS: None, but toilets at Woody's Café for customers
PATHS: Footpaths and by-ways, mostly unsuitable for pushchairs and liable to be (very) muddy after wet spells. Involves a gentle climb and a short stretch along lanes

THE ROUTE: The Recreation Ground has a small children's playground suitable for primary and pre-school children, shady seats and space for a picnic. To start the walk, turn right out of the car park and right at the T-junction then just past the last house go left through a gate to join a 'restricted by-way'. This runs gently uphill at the field boundary but may be muddy and an alternative is a path at the field edge. At the top corner of the field, turn to admire the view over the Pang valley then follow the path ahead into woods (Redhill Copse). Continue along this by-way gently uphill through the woods for about 600m.

Some of the animals in Bucklebury Farm Park ❶ may be glimpsed in fields to the left. Where the by-way levels out, turn sharp left to go through a wooden gate with a public footpath sign and join a path into the Farm Park. Follow this path along a fence at a field edge to a stile. Climb over this and the stile opposite to enter a paddock (maybe with grazing animals!). Cross this diagonally and go through a metal gate at the bottom, then ahead along a paddock edge to another metal gate. Woody's Café, a farm shop and the ticket office for the Farm Park are just ahead on the right. To continue the walk, follow the track ahead then left out of the Park (if the Park is closed, a public footpath runs diagonally across the field to the right of the car park, with a metal gate at each end).

At the entrance to the Farm Park, turn left into Pease Hill and follow this lane gently downhill (keeping an eye open for any traffic). On the right are Bucklebury House, with its fish pond ❷ and Manor Farm. Turn left at the nearby junction (signed Bucklebury) and follow this winding lane. After passing the Old Vicarage on the right, turn right into the churchyard of St Mary's church ❸ by a path next to a cottage (the Old Post Office). Both the exterior and interior of this beautiful church have interesting features and information sheets are available inside. The start of the walk is close to the T-junction just beyond the church.

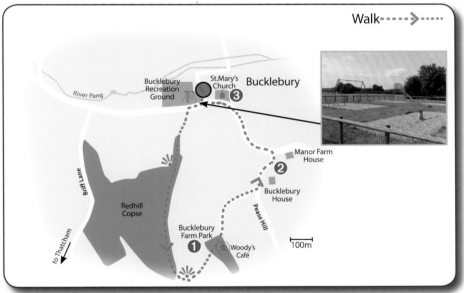

St Mary's Church

Facts and Figures

❶ Set in a 77 acre site, Bucklebury Farm Park has a deer park, farm animals and indoor and outdoor children's play areas. The animals include deer, llamas, alpacas, cattle, goats, sheep, pigs, wild boar, donkeys and ponies. The Park is open daily, except 25 and 26 Dec (see www.buckleburyfarmpark.co.uk).

❷ Bucklebury House is where the extensive Bucklebury Estate is managed. It was formerly known as Bucklebury Old Manor, a Tudor mansion most of which was destroyed by fire in 1833 and not restored until the mid-20th century. An even older manor house once stood here, built for the Abbot of Reading in the 1100s. Nearby is Bucklebury Manor, with an entrance about 500m south along Pease Hill. This Georgian mansion was bought by the Middleton family in 2012 and is, of course, visited by the Duke and Duchess of Cambridge and their children Prince George and Princess Charlotte.

❸ The church of St Mary the Virgin is mainly 12th and 15th century. The south entrance has a richly carved Norman doorway (from about 1150) and the tower (built about 1450) has carved figures halfway up the south-eastern buttress. The interesting artefacts inside include an oak chest with nine locks and crossed iron bands said to be from Reading Abbey, a large wooden board dated 1824 listing church benefactors and six hatchments (diamond-shaped paintings showing the coat of arms and honours of a deceased person, a now-rare custom that began in the 1600s). There are also beautiful stained glass windows; the one by the pew reserved for the Lord of the Manor, on the north side of the church near the pulpit, is well-known for the fly it incorporates. Can you find it?

Bucklebury Farm Park

A stroll from an ancient parish church (the resting place of Agatha Christie) through open fields with wide views and plenty of trains to spot!

START/PARKING: Car park in front of St Mary's church, Church Road, Cholsey, about 5 miles south-east of Didcot (Nat Grid Ref 41/584870, Postcode OX10 9PR)
PUBLIC TRANSPORT: Cholsey rail station about ¾ mile from the start and Thames Travel buses from Wallingford (half-hourly Mon-Fri, hourly Sat and irregular Sun)
DISTANCE: 2 miles (3¼ km)
REFRESHMENTS: The Cholsey Café, open Mon - Sat and Sunday in summer, and Tesco Express, both at The Forty; Red Lion pub, Wallingford Road (www.redlioncholsey.co.uk)
PUBLIC TOILETS: None, but toilets at the Cholsey Café and Red Lion for customers and at the station (when manned).
PATHS: Footpaths and farm tracks; mainly level but liable to be muddy after wet weather and parts unsuitable for pushchairs

THE ROUTE: From the car park, go though the gate into the churchyard of St Mary's church ❶, an attractive flint-faced building. This is best known for the grave of author Agatha Christie ❷, reached by passing the church on your right (note the gargoyles!) and bearing right across the grass towards the far corner. A large headstone marks her resting place and that of her husband Sir Max Mallowan.

Continue to the stile at the corner of the churchyard, from where a path on the right leads across a field towards the buildings of Manor Farm. At the farm track, turn left and follow this down across fields, with open views towards the railway and the rolling Berkshire Downs beyond. Shortly, the track rises through horse chestnut trees to a bridge over the four rail lines, usually busy with freight trains and passenger trains to and from Paddington ❸.

Follow the track down from the bridge through more horse chestnut trees, to pass a farmyard on the right. Shortly, as the farm track bears right, go straight ahead along a grassy path through the fields. Follow this as it bears left along a field edge, with a stream joining on your right. After about 250m this path turns right over a wooden bridge, and continues with a stream to the right.

The path leads to Bulls Hole tunnel under the railway – rather dark with uneven cobbles, so care is needed! Just after this tunnel lies another, much shorter, one - under the single track of the preserved Cholsey to Wallingford railway ❹. Just beyond, turn left to cross a stream by a bridge and follow this path over another small bridge through the Cholsey Millennium Wood, at the edge of which is a plaque to mark the tree planting in 2000. From here, go straight ahead across a sports field to pass a pavilion then turn right over a stream to reach a large recreation ground. There are two children's playgrounds here, one immediately ahead and the other (for younger primary and pre-school children) at the edge of the grass to the right. Plenty of space for picnics.

To continue the walk, at the end of the bridge from the sports field turn left. With the stream on your left, this path leads to Church Road. A short distance to the right is the village centre, The Forty ❺, with a café and supermarket. To complete the walk, turn left at Church Road to pass Cholsey Primary School and climb to the hump-backed bridge over the Cholsey to Wallingford railway. Fine rural views open up, with Manor Farm and the tower of St Mary's church ahead. The car park is soon reached on the left.

St. Mary's Church

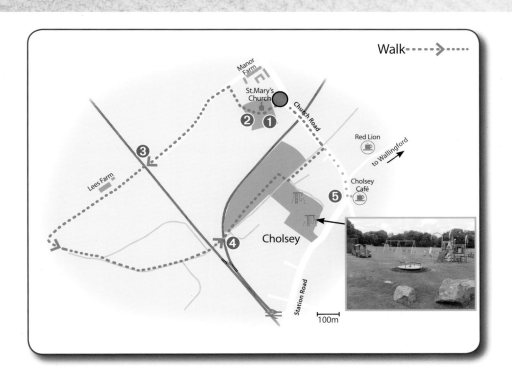

Walk ····> ·····

Wallingford to Cholsey train

Cholsey Station

Facts and Figures

1 Founded as an abbey church in the 10th century, St Mary's was rebuilt between 1150 and 1170. Outside it has remained largely unaltered, retaining its cruciform shape. Notable features include a Norman doorway and a bell cast around 1300.

2 Agatha Christie is the world's bestselling author, having written some 90 books, and her main home from 1934 until her death was Winterbrook House, on the edge of Wallingford (but in the parish of Cholsey). She was married to the archaeologist Sir Max Mallowan. The inscription on the headstone reads 'In Memoriam Agatha Mary Clarissa Mallowan, Agatha Christie Author and Playwright, Born 15th Sept 1890 Died 12th Jan 1976'.

3 The Great Western Railway was built in the mid-19th century to link London with the west of England and Wales. Isambard Kingdom Brunel was appointed engineer and the line he built from Paddington to Bristol had so few gradients it was called 'Brunel's billiard table'. Cholsey first saw trains on 1 June 1840, when the section from Reading to Steventon, just west of Didcot, opened.

4 The 2½ mile Cholsey to Wallingford branch line opened in 1866. Regular passenger services of the 'Wallingford Bunk', as it was affectionately known, ceased in 1959 but the line continued to serve a malt plant at Wallingford until 1981. When this no longer needed the line, the Cholsey and Wallingford Railway Preservation Society was formed. Steam or diesel-hauled heritage trains run on selected weekends and bank holidays (see www.cholsey-wallingford-railway.com).

5 The Forty is the name of the village green, thought to mean 'island in the marshland'. It has magnificent horse chestnut trees and is bordered by attractive cottages.

WALK SIX : GORING-ON-THAMES

See this picturesque riverside village, where the Thames flows through the gap between the rolling Berkshire Downs and Chiltern Hills.

START/PARKING: Wheel Orchard car park, off Station Road, Goring (Nat Grid Ref 41/599807, Postcode RG8 9HB)
PUBLIC TRANSPORT: Goring and Streatley rail station, about ¼ mile from the start and buses from Wallingford, Mon - Sat
DISTANCE: 1 mile (1½ km) or 2 miles (3¼ km)
REFRESHMENTS: Village Café (open daily) and McColl's convenience store (open daily), both in High St; Pierreponts Café near the bridge (open Tues - Sat, www.pierreponts.co.uk); several pubs
PUBLIC TOILETS: At Wheel Orchard car park
PATHS: Pavements and footpaths; level and mainly suitable for pushchairs, although the longer route includes a few short uneven stretches. The riverside path is prone to being flooded when the Thames is high

THE ROUTES: The car park has a village information board. Leave by the footpath at the side of the public toilets and at the end, turn left into the High Street and cross over Manor Road. The garden on the corner here has the Village Sign erected in June 2012 to commemorate the Queen's Golden Jubilee, depicting a red kite flying above the riverside scene. Opposite is the Miller of Mansfield pub ❶. Turn left into Manor Road and shortly right along a path to pass under a gateway into the churchyard of the parish church of St Thomas of Canterbury ❷. With the church on your left, follow the path out of the churchyard and turn right at some wrought iron gates on your left. This narrow lane leads past Mill Cottage on your left and at the end, turn left on to the lower path to the left of where the bridge begins. Pierreponts Café is opposite.

Pass Goring Mill and cross the mill race, then bear right under the bridge ❸ over the grass towards the river. Ahead, water roars over the weir and next to this is Goring Lock, with plenty of passing boats in summer. Return under the bridge to join the Thames Path - a board here gives information about the Goring Gap and the Thames. After crossing a small bridge, follow the riverside path - plenty of benches to pause and take in the fine views of the river and the wooded hills above the opposite bank. Just after crossing a second small bridge, there are two walk options: a short one (via a playground) and a longer, riverside route.

SHORT ROUTE: After crossing the bridge, turn left across a grassed area (possible picnic spot) then follow a footpath into Ferry Lane passing the red-brick RC church on the right. At the end of Ferry Lane, turn left into Manor Road then right into the High Street. This leads to McColl's store on the left and the Village Café on the right. Turn left into Cleeve Road to reach the Gardiner Recreation Ground on the right. There is plenty of space for a picnic and, at the top end, a playground suitable for pre-school children. From here there are wide views over the village to the Berkshire Downs. Then turn right into Upper Red Cross Road, cross the High Street into Red Cross Road, then right into Station Road. Care is needed here as there are no pavements. Fine views again towards the wooded Berkshire hills, and some interesting cottages. At Goring Library, turn right to the Wheel Orchard car park.

RIVERSIDE ROUTE: Follow the path along the Thames, with fields on the left, as far as a metal gate. Here, fine views of the rolling Chilterns open up, with the railway from Paddington to the west in the middle distance. Take the path that curves left across a grassy field to reach a wooden gate. From here, go straight ahead along a stony track and at the T-junction at the end of this, turn left past a gate. This wider track leads to Manor Road. Follow this leafy residential road back into the village, then either turn right into Station Road to go directly to the car park or next right into the High Street for refreshments and a children's playground (see short route).

Boathouse near Goring Lock

Village Sign

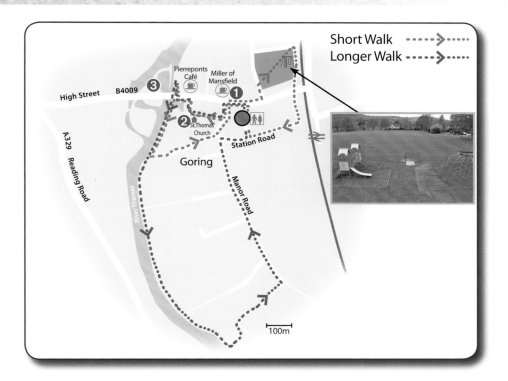

Facts and Figures

❶ This 18th century coaching inn is named after an old English ballad 'King Henry II and the Miller of Mansfield'. This tells of a Nottinghamshire miller who entertained the King at his house, including a supper of venison from a poached royal deer!

❷ The church of St Thomas of Canterbury dates back to the 11th century, but was re-modelled in 1886. A fine carved wooden altar screen dominates the simple, spacious interior. A bell cast in about 1290 – one of the oldest inscribed bells in England – hangs inside on the west wall of the church.

❸ Before a toll bridge was built in 1837, the river crossing was by boat from Ferry Lane. The present bridge was built in 1923, when tolls were abolished. On 3 June 2012, the bridge was at the centre of the largest Diamond Jubilee street party in the UK, attended by over 4000 people and stretching over half a mile from Goring to Streatley.

WALK SEVEN : HAMPSTEAD NORREYS

A ramble round this pretty village on the upper reaches of the River Pang, through ancient woodland to the remains of a Norman castle.

START/PARKING: Village Hall car park, off the B4009 Streatley to Newbury road at the western edge of Hampstead Norreys (Nat Grid Ref 41/527763, postcode RG18 0TR)
PUBLIC TRANSPORT: Buses from Newbury (services 6/6A Mon-Sat)
DISTANCE: 1¼ miles (2 km)
REFRESHMENTS: Hampstead Norreys Community Shop (open Mon - Sat and Sun morning); White Hart inn, with a garden (closed Mon, www.goodfoodatthewhitehart.co.uk)
PUBLIC TOILETS: None, but toilets at the White Hart for customers
PATHS: Mostly footpaths and bridleways, liable to be muddy after wet weather and unsuitable for pushchairs

THE ROUTE: The Village Hall car park is next to Dean Meadow, where there is a well-equipped children's playground, an 'outdoor gym' for teenagers and adults, seats and plenty of space for a picnic.

For the walk, go through the playground to a gate in the corner and turn right on to a public bridleway. Close by is an information board about Hampstead Norreys Motte, which will be reached shortly ❶. At the nearby farm entrance, follow the footpath ahead gently uphill into the woods and at the next junction of paths, again take the path straight ahead. Shortly, on the right is a sign for the Motte, the remains of which will be found by following the small path past the sign (a short, steep climb leads to the top of the mound). The surrounding woods, Westbrook Copse, are criss-crossed by paths.

At the path junction close to the Motte sign, take the one to the left leading gently downhill. Where this meets a wider path, take the narrow path ahead (slightly to the right). This leads to a metal gate and across a meadow to the River Pang ❷ - picnic and (probably) paddling opportunities here! Then retrace your steps through the gate, up the slope and turn right on to the wider path. This leads back to the edge of the woods, with Manor Farm on the right. By the gate to Dean Meadow, turn right on to the path into the churchyard of the beautiful St Mary's parish church ❸.

Turn right into Church Street, which leads to Manor Courtyard on the right with a Community Shop selling drinks and ice creams. Carefully cross the road here and continue along Church Street. Pass the old village well on the left and then cross the Pang, to reach the attractive 16th century White Hart inn.

At the corner, where Forge Hill begins, turn left on to a track. About 70m beyond farm buildings on the left, before a farm gate, a footpath crosses this track. To the right leads uphill along a field boundary and provides fine views over the village and Pang valley but, to continue the walk, turn left and cross a field to reach cottages and a narrow lane. Follow this, crossing a small bridge over the Pang, to a road (Water Street). Cross this to go up The Close almost opposite and at the top, by no 15, turn left on to a footpath. Follow this path (the route of the former Didcot to Newbury railway) to pass under a bridge and reach the start of the walk on the left.

Close by on the B4009 towards Streatley is The Living Rainforest with glasshouses containing 700 species of tropical plants and animals (www.livingrainforest.org)

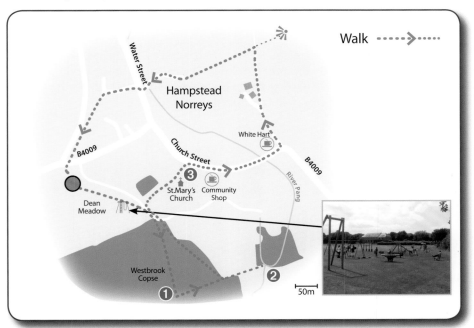

Facts and Figures

❶ A motte was an early type of castle built by the Normans in the 11th century, consisting of an earth mound, a timber fence and timber tower. Little is known about the one at Hampstead Norreys but at the time of the Domesday Survey, the manor was owned by Theodoric the Goldsmith and he may have built it to protect his stores of metal and jewels. Trees now obscure the view it once commanded and only the earth mound remains. However, some consider this to be a Bronze Age burial mound, so its origin is somewhat controversial!

❷ The Pang is a chalk stream that normally rises high in the Berkshire Downs near Compton and East Ilsley and flows south then east and north-east for about 14 miles to join the Thames at Pangbourne. The flow is uncertain in its upper reaches, being dependent on the underlying water table. At Hampstead Norreys it typically flows from mid-winter to early autumn, but this pattern is disrupted by prolonged wet or dry spells – it dried up in summer 2004 for 2½ years!

❸ St Mary's church has a distinctive flintwork tower with cream limewash and is substantially 12th and 13th century, with later additions. It contains ancient decoration including a carved stone knight on horseback, thought to be late 12th century. An information sheet describes this and other notable features. A blue plaque on the churchyard wall records the village's entry in the Domesday Book of 1086 when it was known as Hanstede, a farm settlement in early English. It became Hampstead Norreys in the 1400s, when the Norreys family acquired the manor.

St.Mary's Church   The White Hart

From the Thames river meadows at Pangbourne over a toll bridge to the picturesque village of Whitchurch-on-Thames.

START/PARKING: Pangbourne Recreation Ground car park (free), on the left at the end of Thames Avenue off B471 Whitchurch Road, Pangbourne (Nat Grid Ref 41/637767, Postcode RG8 7BU). Alternative pay and display parking nearby at the River Meadow and Working Men's Club car parks, both off B471 Whitchurch Road

PUBLIC TRANSPORT: Pangbourne rail station, about ¼ mile from start; Thames Travel buses from Reading, Mon - Sat

DISTANCE: 1 mile (1½ km) or 2 miles (3¼ km)

REFRESHMENTS: Several cafés and pubs in Pangbourne; The Ferryboat (closed Mon) and Greyhound pubs in Whitchurch

PUBLIC TOILETS: Recreation Ground car park (8am to 6pm)

PATHS: Pavements and footpaths including riverside; level and suitable for pushchairs. Pangbourne Meadow can be muddy after wet weather (and is prone to being flooded when the Thames is high)

THE ROUTES: From the children's playground at the recreation ground, head towards the Thames across Pangbourne Meadow ❶. There is usually something to see on the river here – boats, swans, ducks and canoe lessons. There are plenty of seats and space for picnics.

From the meadow, go through the gate near Dolphin House ❷ then carefully cross the road at the end of Whitchurch toll bridge ❸. Cross the bridge, admiring the views up- and down-stream including Whitchurch lock and the mill pond with the church beyond. On the wall of the toll house on the left there is an information board and a replica list of 'tolls to be taken at this gate' dating from 1792. By the toll gate, turn left into the lane towards the Mill then, just past Church Cottages, turn right into a narrow walled path. This leads to the flint-faced parish church of St Mary the Virgin ❹. At the far side of the churchyard, bear right along the tarmac drive to rejoin the High Street. For the shorter walk, turn right here to return to the bridge or, to explore more of this picturesque village, turn left up the High Street. An information board on the wall opposite the Greyhound pub describes the key buildings. Another children's playground (suitable for primary and pre-school children) will be found a short distance along Manor Road, the next turning on the left. Shortly after Manor Road, carefully cross the High Street and take the next turning on the right, Hardwick Road. Follow this to the edge of the village then, opposite a house called 'Primrose Hill', turn right down a broad public footpath. On the left, within a wildflower meadow, is the (mystical) Whitchurch Maze with an information board ❺. The path leads gently downhill past the Village Green playing field on the right (with benches and space for picnics). At the end, turn right into Eastfield Lane and follow this back to the High Street. Turn left here to return to the toll bridge and the start of the walk.

Pangbourne has a good range of shops, many of them independent, and the historic parish church of St James the Less. Next to the church is Church Cottage, the former home of Kenneth Grahame, author of 'The Wind in the Willows'.

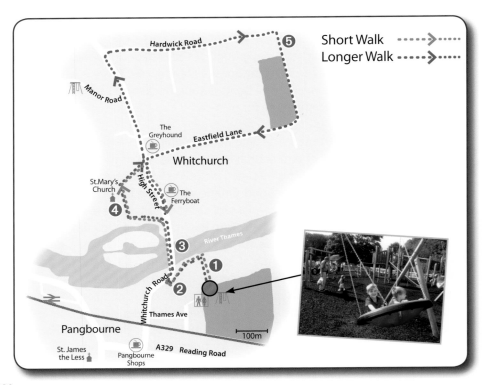

Facts and Figures

❶ Pangbourne Meadow is owned by the Parish Council and the adjacent six acres of land downstream by the National Trust. The reach of the Thames from here downstream could easily be home to Mole, Ratty and friends from 'The Wind in the Willows' whose author, Kenneth Grahame, lived in Pangbourne from 1924 to 1932.

❷ Dolphin House is one of three Adventure Dolphin centres in West Berkshire, for training people in outdoor activities. Those involving water, such as kayaking and canoeing, take place here. The centre is named after John Dolphin who, as chairman of Pangbourne Athletic Club, raised funds for a youth centre that opened in 1961, being replaced by the present building in 2010.

❸ Whitchurch bridge is one of only two toll bridges on the non-tidal Thames, the other being at Eynsham near Oxford. It is used by around 5,000 vehicles most weekdays. The first toll bridge was built in 1792 and replaced in 1853. Both these bridges were wooden and an iron one was built in 1901-02. This was re-built in 2013-14.

❹ The original church, built of chalk rubble and flint, gave its name to the village – 'Hwitcurke' (white church). It was replaced by a Norman building, but restoration in the mid-19th century retained only the Norman south porch. There are some beautiful stained glass windows and inside, on the south wall, a fine monument to Richard Lybbe (1525 - 1599) and his wife, both kneeling.

❺ The maze was created in 2004 using concentric circles of bricks, many engraved with family names, dates and events. At the centre is a sundial to tell the time by the shadow of a person standing on the initial of the current month. L-shaped metal divining rods may be used to find energy fields under the starting point and centre of the maze – giving a somewhat mystical air to the site.

Whitchurch Bridge

River Thames from the Meadow

9

Watch boats pass through a lock in a scenic setting and stroll along the Thames with views of historic Mapledurham.

START/PARKING: Roadside in Purley Village, reached from A329 Reading to Pangbourne road via either New Hill or Purley Lane (Nat Grid Ref 41/664762, Postcode RG8 8AX)
PUBLIC TRANSPORT: Reading Buses route 16 from Reading daily, and Thames Travel buses along Reading Road, Mon - Sat
DISTANCE: 1½ miles (2½ km)
REFRESHMENTS: Café at Mapledurham Lock (usually open 10am to 5pm daily from Easter to the end of October and at weekends in winter)
PUBLIC TOILETS: At Mapledurham Lock
PATHS: Roads and footpaths; level. Suitable for pushchairs, but riverside path liable to be muddy after wet weather (and prone to being flooded when the Thames is high)

THE ROUTE: From Purley Village, with fields on your left, turn left into Mapledurham Drive (single track road). There are open views ahead to the Chilterns. After passing through a gate, another on the left leads to Bucknell's Meadow, which has a children's playground and an 'outdoor gym' for ages 10 upwards. There are seats and plenty of space for picnics. Continue along the gravel road then bear right through a gate (just before a cattle grid). Go straight ahead across the field, towards a weir on the Thames. A gate on the left leads to Mapledurham Lock ❶, in a beautiful setting with the rolling Chilterns countryside as a backdrop. Plenty of seats to admire the views and watch any boats passing through the lock, and the Lock Café. A board gives information about the lock and the Thames. Just beyond the first gate upstream of the lock is a boules piste, a stony area for playing this traditional French game.

Retrace your steps through the gate downstream of the lock and, after admiring the white water roaring over the weir, follow the riverside path through the broad river meadow. Soon, there are glimpses through the trees of the small village of Mapledurham on the opposite bank with its watermill, church and manor house ❷. Follow the riverside path as far as a gate to a road (River Gardens) beyond. From here, either retrace your steps along the riverbank to return to Mapledurham Drive, or from River Gardens take the first road on the right into Wintringham Way ❸. Go straight ahead along this residential road to a gate that leads into Mapledurham Drive, then turn left and return to the start at Purley Village.

Heading upstream

Mapledurham House

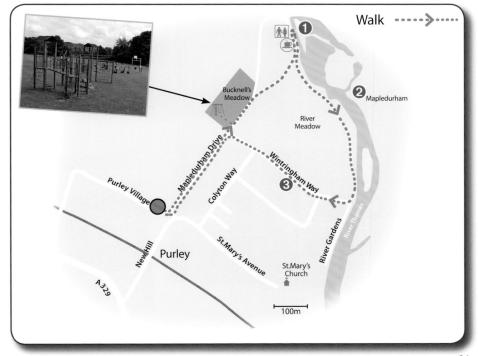

Facts and Figures

❶ Mapledurham Lock is 78½ miles from London and 33 miles from Oxford, by river. A pound lock was first built here in 1777 and the present one dates from 1908. It was the first on the Thames to be mechanised, in 1956. The adjacent weir is the furthest upstream with a salmon ladder. Marks on the wall just upstream of the lock record the river levels in the floods of 1894, 1947 and 2003. The river meadows and parts of Purley village were also badly flooded in early 2014.

❷ The Mapledurham estate has been owned by the Blount family since the late 1400s. St Margaret's church dates from the late 13th century and red-brick Mapledurham House was completed in 1612. A watermill here was mentioned in the Domesday Survey of 1086 and this mill, dating from the 1400s, is now the oldest working mill on the Thames, producing stone-ground flour. This relatively remote village has been used as a set for several films, most notably as a Second World War battlefield for the 1976 film 'The Eagle Has Landed'.

❸ In the 1930s, land near the river was sold to campers for £5 a plot and these plots were used by Londoners as a weekend retreat. During and immediately after the Second World War, these plots began to be occupied permanently and the 'homes' were often old railway carriages, buses or huts. Many of these suffered badly in the floods of 1947 and since then they have been progressively replaced by brick-built houses; a few old bungalows still remain in Mapledurham Drive and Wintringham Way.

Lock & Weir

MAPLEDURHAM
TO
LONDON
78½ MILES
TO
OXFORD
33 MILES

10 WALK TEN: THATCHAM LAKE

See and learn about the abundant wildlife of Thatcham Lake and the neighbouring reedbeds.

START/PARKING: Car park (donations welcomed) at the Nature Discovery Centre, off Lower Way, Thatcham (Nat Grid Ref 41/506671, Postcode RG19 3FU)
PUBLIC TRANSPORT: Newbury & District buses from Newbury, Mon-Sat and Reading buses from Newbury and Reading, daily
DISTANCE: ¾ mile (1¼ km)
REFRESHMENTS: Lakeside Café in the Discovery Centre (closed Mon, Nov-Feb)
PUBLIC TOILETS: At the Discovery Centre
PATHS: Footpaths; level and suitable for pushchairs but liable to be muddy after wet weather

THE ROUTE: Next to the car park are two playgrounds – one suitable for pre-school and younger primary school children and one for older children. Just beyond is the Nature Discovery Centre, overlooking the lake ❶. This has a café and an information centre, with interactive natural history displays, giant jigsaw puzzles, wildlife brass rubbings and a shop with wildlife-related gifts. It is usually open daily from March to October but closed on Monday in the winter (see www.bbowt.org.uk). The Centre is a popular venue for family-based events and school groups visiting for environmental education activities. It sells bags of food for the many water birds on the adjacent lake and there are usually plenty of hungry beaks on the water just by the Centre! Information boards, with a map of the lake and reedbeds, will be found near the playgrounds and by the lake to the right of the Centre.

For a short walk, from the Centre follow the lakeside path either clockwise or anti-clockwise around the lake. There are plenty of places for a picnic and benches to pause and spot the birds ❷. For a longer walk, at the far end of the lake public footpaths lead through the Thatcham Reedbed Nature Reserve ❸ to the Kennet and Avon canal. There is an open water and wetland trail to follow (about an extra 1¾ miles) with blue waymarking posts - note that at one point this involves crossing railway tracks.

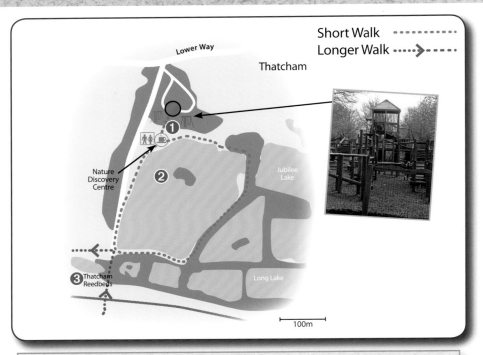

Facts and Figures

❶ The Nature Discovery Centre opened in 1995 and was extended in 2007. It is managed by the Berks, Bucks and Oxon Wildlife Trust on behalf of West Berkshire Council. The lake is one of a series created by gravel extraction in the 1970s and landscaped in the mid-1980s. Today the lake and surrounding area, with its variety of habitats, are teeming with wildlife - something to see all year round.

❷ Typically about 20 species of birds may be seen on and around the lake throughout the year. The numbers are swelled in winter and early spring by migrant visitors. Species include great crested grebes with their amazing courtship ritual in spring, reed warblers that cling to reed stems as they sing and sand martins that excavate nest tunnels in sandy banks. In summer, common terns nest on the tern raft in the lake.

❸ This 165 acre wetland habitat is one of the largest areas of inland reedbeds in Southern England and home to a number of rare and/or threatened species of plants and animals. Thatcham gets its name from the reeds that used to be cut for thatching.

Lake & Discovery Centre

Great Crested Grebe

Moorhen

Cormorant

Mute Swan

Kingfisher

Tufted Duck

Pochard

Mallard

From the bustling High Street, with reminders of the old coaching road to Bath, to the quiet hamlet of North Street.

START/PARKING: Car park (free) at the Village Hall, Englefield Road, Theale, off the A4 just west of junction 12 of the M4 (Nat Grid Ref 41/638715, Postcode RG7 5AS)
PUBLIC TRANSPORT: Reading to Newbury buses; Theale rail station about ¼ mile from village centre
DISTANCE: 2 miles (3¼ km)
REFRESHMENTS: Various pubs, cafés and convenience stores in Theale High Street
PUBLIC TOILETS: None, but toilets at the pubs for customers
PATHS: Footpaths and pavements; level and mostly suitable for pushchairs. A short stretch along a lane

THE ROUTE: From the car park, cross the sports field towards the church. At the far side is a playground, suitable for pre-school and younger primary age children. Leave the sports field by a gravel path in the corner, into the graveyard and grounds of the imposing Holy Trinity church ❶. Follow the path under its bell tower and turn left into Church Street – a Victorian post box is in the wall here. Cross Englefield Road and, at the mini-roundabout, cross Crown Lane and go ahead into the High Street ❷. This has an attractive mix of shops, businesses, 18th and 19th century houses and cottages and three pubs (old coaching inns) – the Crown Inn, the Falcon and the Bull. Next to the Bull is Brewery Court, the surviving buildings of a former brewery ❸.

Continue ahead at the next mini-roundabout, and turn left into Woodfield Way. Go through this small housing estate to reach an open area on the right. Here, take the footpath to the left and follow this to reach a narrow lane near a pair of cottages. Turn right here and follow the lane to a corner by a cottage, where a grassy path begins on the left by a metal gate. Follow this between hedges to reach the edge of Theale Golf Centre. A public footpath crosses the golf course, but keep an eye open for any balls! The path goes ahead past a large oak tree on the right, to a pair of wooden posts and through a small coppice. It then bears left across the fairways towards two further pairs of wooden posts, then ahead past two oaks (on right) to reach a metal gate. Here, turn right on to a metalled path leading to a narrow lane. Turning right here leads into the hamlet of North Street with a variety of old houses and cottages, some thatched. A shady bench ('Millennium seat') at the far end provides somewhere to rest at the half-way point.

From North Street, retrace your steps to the metalled footpath, now on the left, and follow this with the golf course on your left. A few metres after crossing the road into the Golf Centre, turn right through a gap in a fence into a large playing field. Head across this to the opposite corner, where a gate leads to Englefield Road and the start of the walk.

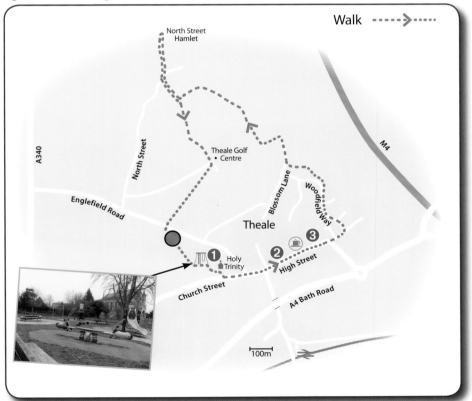

Facts and Figures

1 The parish church of Holy Trinity was completed in 1832 in the early English style. It has a cathedral-like stature and aspects of the design are said to have been inspired by Salisbury Cathedral.

2 Theale was an important staging post for coaches and horse traffic on the London to Bath road. In the early 19th century, there were 11 coaching inns along the High Street and Church Street, together with shops and tradesmen serving the needs of travellers and their horses. The advent of the railway in the early 1840s led to a decline in coach traffic. However, five of the inns survive, a good example being the early 18th century 'Falcon' with an archway into its coaching yard.

3 In the 1700s, maltings on this site provided malt for home brewing. In the early 19th century, a brewery was established here and in 1854 this was bought by the Blatch family. It remained in their ownership until 1965, after which it closed. The remaining attractive red brick buildings, including the malt house, are now used for offices - Brewery Court.

Holy Trinity Church

North Street

12

Discover this peaceful village nestled in an area of the Berkshire Downs famous for racehorses and sheep.

START/PARKING: At the start of the bridleway off the western end of Main Street, West Ilsley which is close to the A34 between Newbury and Didcot (Nat Grid Ref 41/470826, Postcode RG20 7AR)
PUBLIC TRANSPORT: Buses from Newbury (services 6/6A, Mon - Sat)
DISTANCE: 1½ miles (2½ km)
REFRESHMENTS: The Harrow pub, with gardens, open daily 12-3pm and from 6pm (www.theharrowwestilsley.com)
PUBLIC TOILETS: None, but toilets at The Harrow for customers
PATHS: Footpaths and pavements, mostly level but the footpaths are unsuitable for pushchairs

THE ROUTE: From the bridleway, turn left into Main Street to pass the Harrow pub on the left. This looks across to the cricket field, in the south-west corner of which is a well-equipped children's playground. To reach this, go up Catmore Road opposite the Harrow and through the gate by the cricket pavilion. Also close to the Harrow is the village pond, with its resident ducks and a gazebo erected to mark the new millennium that incorporates maps of the local area.

From the pond, continue along Main Street, with its attractive cottages, the Village Hall and old School House. Carefully cross Bury Lane, to pass the lychgate of the parish church of All Saints ❶ on the right. Continue along Main Street and just past Morland Close is a wall with a first floor bay window – this is part of historic West Ilsley House ❷. Here, cross the road to take a gravel by-way signed Church Way on the right. Follow this between houses to reach a lane. On the right are the gates of Keeper's Stables, with horses here and in the nearby fields, and the lane to the right leads to West Ilsley Stables ❸.

To continue the walk, at the end of Church Way take the lane to the left to return to Main Street. Cross this, turn right then at the edge of the village turn left on to a 'restricted by-way'. After passing cottages, the track divides just before a thatched cottage. Take the left hand track and, where a bridleway leaves on the right, take the footpath curving left around the cottage garden. Follow this path along the field boundary, with fine views of the rolling downland fields to the north and over the village to the south. The only sounds you are likely to hear are birds, sheep and horses! The path leads past a farm barn to Bury Lane. Carefully cross this to the track opposite and follow the footpath ahead. At a path junction, turn right across a stile and join a wide grassy track. There is a view of the pond below to the left. This track leads to a stile and a few steps down to a bridleway. Turn left to return to the start and the Harrow pub.

For longer circular walks, the bridleways at each end of Main Street lead up to the Ridgeway, about 1 mile to the north, with its spectacular views (Walk 2, page 9 has facts and figures about the Ridgeway).

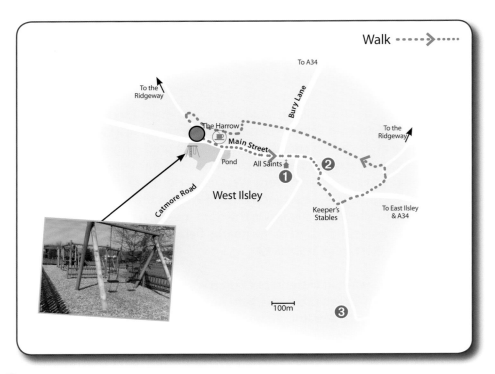

Facts and Figures

❶ The flint-faced All Saints church was remodelled in the late 1800s and almost no trace of its 12th century origins remains.

❷ West Ilsley House was the home of John Morland, a farmer who founded a brewery in the village in 1711. The Morland brewery re-located to Abingdon in 1887 and operated there until 2000 when it was bought by Greene King. There are reminders of the brewery in the nearby road names Morland Close and The Maltings.

❸ Racehorses have been trained at the West Ilsley Stables since the early 1900s, the stables being owned by HM The Queen from 1982 to 1999. Ownership then transferred to Mick Channon, who now trains well over 150 horses. These use gallops here and on Hodcott Down, Sheep Down and the Ridgeway just north of the village, the springy turf of the chalky downs being ideal for racehorses. In centuries past, sheep-rearing dominated the area, with large flocks being driven to the famous sheep fairs at nearby East Ilsley.

The Harrow

Cricket Scoreboard

41

Further Information

Some useful websites to help you plan and enjoy the walks.

MET OFFICE
www.metoffice.gov.uk
Local weather forecasts for 1 to 5 days ahead.

ORDNANCE SURVEY
www.ordnancesurvey.co.uk
Mapping services, including online access to Landranger and Pathfinder maps.

THAMES TRAVEL BUSES
www.thames-travel.co.uk/timetables-fares/
Maps and timetables for buses in South Oxon and West Berkshire.

NEWBURY AND DISTRICT BUSES
www.newburyanddistrict.co.uk
Timetables for buses in West Berkshire.

GREAT WESTERN RAILWAY TRAINS
www.gwr.com
Timetables, tickets and train running information.

KENNET AND AVON CANAL TRUST
www.katrust.org.uk
History of the canal, events and boat trips.

NORTH WESSEX DOWNS AREA OF OUTSTANDING NATURAL BEAUTY(AONB)
www.northwessexdowns.org.uk
Visitor guide, maps, news and events across the AONB.

BERKS, BUCKS AND OXON WILDLIFE TRUST
www.bbowt.org.uk
Nature reserves, events and wildlife information.

WEST BERKSHIRE COUNTRYSIDE SOCIETY
www.westberkscountryside.org.uk
Promotion and conservation of the landscape and wildlife of the West Berkshire countryside.

GEOCACHING
www.geocaching.com
Treasure hunting using a GPS receiver to seek hidden small containers with logbooks and items such as toys and trinkets. There are 'geocaches' on or close to all the walks.